Grammarlocks
and the
Three Theiyr'res

an elementary through adult adventure

Twisted Tales from Atop Gram'mar Mountain
Illustrating the rules of basic grammar,
one twisted fairy tale at a time.

Written by **Rod A. Galindo**
Illustrated by **Brittany Penn**

WHISKERS

an imprint of **Wordwraith Books**

ISBN: 978-1-946921-05-5

Whiskers, an imprint of Wordwraith Books, LLC
705-B SE Melody Lane #147
Lee's Summit, MO 64063
www.wordwraithbooks.com
@Wordwraiths

Tales from Atop Grammar Mountain: www.grammarmountain.com

Cover art by Brittany Penn
Brittany's website: https://brittanyvonnepenn.wixsite.com/portfolio/
Contact Brittany: bypenn.art@gmail.com

Rod's website www.rodgalindo.com
Contact Rod: rod@rodwerks.net

PARENTS!
USE CARE WHEN READING
THIS BOOK ALOUD

If you read Grammarlocks aloud when your listener **can't see the text**, its reason for existing can be lost. If you haven't already realized, the sound all the "key" words make are phonetically the same. *But I have a solution!*

Grab three pieces of paper. Write one of the following words on each page.

THERE   THEIR   THEY'RE

Now have the listener hold up the correct word when you come across it in the story. This works both for an audience (fun) or when it's just you and your ~~co-worker~~ child (educational).

Happy learning! Or refreshing important skills, whichever the case may be.

- Rod

Grammarlocks

and the

Three Theiyr'res

Once upon a time, **there** lived three civilized *theiyr'res* in a small cottage up on Gram'mar Mountain.

A Papa **There**,
a Mama **Their**,
and a Baby **They're**.

1

One day, while the Three
Theiyr'res were down in the valley at
Baby's spelling bee, a sweet but angry little diva named
Grammarlocks happened upon their cabin after a fight with
her boyfriend.

She pounded three times on the big wooden door. No answer. Before her was a welcome mat sporting large, friendly letters. It read, "GO AWAY." She smirked, lifted the mat, snatched the spare key, and let herself in.

"Hellooo?" she called. Silence. Grammarlocks zipped up the wide staircase wearing a sweet smile.

At the top of the stairs she found a door to the left, and a door to the right. "Eenie, meenie, miney... mo." She spun to the right, and cranked the huge doorknob.

A bear-sized bed loomed before her, just begging to be bounced upon. "This must be Papa **There** and Mama **Their's** room!"

4

She took a running leap and landed hard on Papa's side of the bed. "This thing is hard as Plymouth Rock!"

She rolled over onto Mama **Their's** side and was nearly swallowed by the comforter. "Woah! What is this, a Nap Number bed!?"

Grammarlocks tumbled off the high mattress and onto the floor, banging her knee. "Owie!" she yelped. "I hate this room!" And she stomped out.

She barreled through the only other door on this floor, and found a bed more her size.

"Yay, Baby **They're's** bed!" And she bounced and bounced until her bouncer was broken.

"Whew, I'm tired!" she exclaimed, and plopped down on the pillow. Soon, she got that little crinkle between her eyes, and her lower lip jutted out in a frustrated pout. "Geez, this bed isn't even close to 'just right'! These bears must have serious back problems!"

Grammarlocks sat up on her elbows. To her surprise, all the covers were on the floor. "Uh oh. **They're** going to be maaad." She flipped her hair and shrugged. "Eh, no biggie. I'm hungry."

Grammarlocks slid down the bannister and sailed into the kitchen. She skidded to a halt before a big wooden dinner table. Three chairs were set around it, and three bowls were set upon it. Each bowl was partially filled with alphabet soup.

She climbed up onto the largest chair and peered into the lettery chaos before her. "This must be Papa **There's** soup!" The spoon was too big to fit into her porridge-hole, so she just picked up the big round thing and put it to her tiny mouth.

Grammarlocks twisted her face and stuck out her tongue. "Ugh. This soup is too... *location-y!*" She thought about running away to another forest, thinking it might be better **there**, but for now she was satisfied with just moving over to the medium-sized chair.

She decided the medium-sized bowl before the medium-sized chair belonged to Mama **Their**. Grammarlocks took a sip.

Her eyes narrowed and she slammed her fist on the table. "Yuck! This one is *too possessive!*"

Grammarlocks pulled out her færiPhone and immediately sent her boyfriend a curt text message.

She then updated her *Facebark* status to "Single."

11

While she was at it, she checked-in at her current location...

Grammarlocks then climbed over to the next bowl. This one was tiny for a fully grown bear, but just right for a sweet little angel like herself. The spoon was just right, too. "This soup must belong to Baby **They're!**"

She took a sip and made a face. "Well, **they're** all pretty terrible, but I'm *contraction-ally* obligated to eat something!" So she slurped and slurped until there was not another drop.

Her tummy now full, she stared at the empty bowl.
"Oh boy. **They're** gonna be soooo mad!"

She flipped her hair and shrugged.
"Eh, no biggie. I'm tired."

Grammarlocks yawned, poured herself onto the downright hideous red sofa in the living room, and was soon fast asleep.

She had restless dreams of angels with confusing angles.

Down in the valley, Papa **There** tried his best not to stink up the spelling bee. Failing miserably, he politely excused himself to do his business in the woods.

He found a quiet, shady spot and settled in. He unlocked his færiPhone with his resting scowl face, because his paws were just too darn big for the bio sensor.

Upon opening *Facebark*, he roared at various jokes and racoon videos, and reeled in horror at the *grim* tales his fellow fairy tale critters had posted overnight.

Scrolling further, Papa **There's** big brown eyes finally fell upon Grammarlocks' new status...

Papa finished up, shoved the roll of Chœrmin back on the tree, and galloped back to the spelling bee.

When he returned, he learned Baby had misspelled "American Psychological Association" in the third round. But Mama **Their** insisted he had gone out with *style*.

It was dark when the Three Theiyr'res arrived at **their** cottage. Every lamp was on, and the front door was ajar.

"I told you that spare key was a security risk," whispered Mama.

Just as Papa had predicted, **there** was the annoying little Grammar devil on **their** sofa, snoring softly. **Their** key and a pink fœriPhone lay on the kitchen table beside Baby **They're's** bowl.

Mama rushed to the phone on the wall and called the **Grammar Police.**

Papa paced back and forth in front of the couch on all fours. "Well, Mama? Are the GPs coming to get this little trespasser?"

"**They're** on the other side of the mountain right now," she replied. "It's another *Youer'r* emergency."

Papa reared up on his haunches. "Hang up the phone, Mama. **THEY'RE** not needed. This time, **THEIR** presence is not required. For all I care, the GPs can stay forever over **THERE**, says *this* bear!"

Grammarlocks awoke at Papa's outburst, and the family of theiyr're bears gathered 'round.

"Mama," whispered Papa **There**, with a deadly stare, "close the curtains."

22

And the Three Theiyr'res ate Grammarlocks right **there** on the spot. She wasn't sugar and spice and everything nice, but even *bad Grammar* is better than cold alphabet soup any day.

The

End

The Three Theiyr'res will return.

About the Author

Rod A. Galindo is a child of the '70s and '80s. He holds a B. A. in Psychology from the University of Kansas, and will probably work for the U.S. Government 'till the end of his days. Two of his offspring are cyber-smart teenaged boys to whom he goes for all technical quandaries, and the other is a sharp-witted German Army (Bundeswehr) Soldatin who is as dangerously clever as she is beautiful. He also fills in as full-time father to a special little social butterfly who never really had a dad to call her own.

"Major" Galindo (retired) has nearly thirty years of service under his belt in the U. S. Army, both Active Duty and in the Kansas Army National Guard. As both an enlisted man and an artillery officer, he has served in Operation Desert Storm in Saudi Arabia, Kuwait, and Iraq, Operation Noble Eagle in Kansas, Operation Iraqi Freedom in Iraq, and Operation Inherent Resolve in the Hashemite Kingdom of Jordan.

Rod has traveled all over the planet and back again, but calls Kansas City home. Enjoy his shiny art or delve into his literary musings at RodWerks.net or RodGalindo.com.

About the Illustrator

Brittany Penn earned a Bachelor of Fine Arts degree from The School of The Art Institute of Chicago in 2012 with a focus in Fine Arts and Video Production. She later earned a Master of Fine Arts degree from the Academy of Art University in 2017, majoring in 2D traditional animation.

She currently works as a remote freelance illustrator, character designer, and animator. While juggling children's book illustration projects, she often works as a 2D animation assistant & production artist producing 2D animated music videos and stage visuals for touring bands.

Find Brittany online at https://brittanyyvonnepenn.wixsite.com/portfolio/ or email her at bypenn.art@gmail.com

A Note from the Author for educators, parents, and the "older" kids

1. There are many, *many* books on English grammar, and if you stack them all in a pile at the center of a room full of English professors, I suggest you run. Because if you stay, you'll likely witness an argument or even fisticuffs as they debate the finer technical points of traditional vs. modernized English, English vs. Latin constructions, etc. This book is more simple, written by a former soldier with a mere bachelor's in Psychology, but sporting a doctorate in sci fi and pop culture (self-awarded). Custodianship of the English language is a hobby of mine, one I thoroughly enjoy. I respect English, and hate to see it used carelessly. "Words and phrases mean things!" you may have heard someone exclaim. That's because they do. The precise use of any language is necessary to avoid confusion, misunderstandings, and arguments. This book reflects accepted rules of written English outlined in various references easily found in libraries and online, such as Strunk and White's classic, *Elements of Style (1959)*, and the unflappable Mignon "Grammar Girl" Fogarty's Quick and Dirty Tips network (here's her URL: https://www.quickanddirtytips.com/grammar-girl). I will never pretend to be a Bas Aarts (I've never even been to London), nor do I have the education/knowledge to argue with those who have read Quirk, Greenbaum, Leech, and Svartvik's *Comprehensive Grammar of the English Language* cover to cover, or even Huddleston and Pullum's Cambridge Grammar of the English Language. So, in this book, you may find nuances of grammar you don't agree with, and indeed some creative license has been taken for artistic and stylistic purposes. I strive for a 90% or better solution of accuracy, however, meaning, if you take away *something* from a Gram'mar Mountain book, you will hopefully be *this much* better armed for that briefing you have to present to your supervisor. But if you're an English teacher or a journalist, you might want to verify your question with other references. I therefore want to apologize in advance for offending any serious students of advanced English, but most "errors" in this book were done intentionally. I think Mr. Aarts would agree with me on my cavalier splitting of infinitives (us mere mortals use them daily in regular speech, e-mail, and social media posts, after all), but I am still struggling with his decision to use the pronoun "they" vice "he or she" after an identifier like "someone". And yes, I probably could have put the period inside the quotes at the end of the previous sentence—because putting it outside often looks odd—but this is an example of where I decided to put accuracy ahead of style.

2. If you find something in these pages that you think is incorrect (at the time of publication, not in 2050 after the language has evolved significantly or anything), don't hesitate to let me know! But please, research the supposed error in no less than three reputable publications first. Things may have changed since you were in school; a lot has changed since *I* learned reading, writing, and 'rithmetic, and many things my wonderful teachers drilled into my noggin that were correct in the mid-to-late 20th Century are frowned upon today. For instance, don't try to type two spaces after a period around a millennial (or any post Gen-Xer) for that matter. You've been warned. Edit: A quick Find & Replace found over two dozen double spaces on this page alone after I had finished typing it up. Old habits die hard.

3. You may find a lovely *interrobang* at the end of sentences in certain circumstances. That's the "!?" or "‽" symbol. Although this is not an officially accepted punctuation mark in the formal English world, I maintain that it should be, and here are three examples to illustrate why:

   "What?" she exclaimed.
   "What!" she asked.
   "What!?"

   The last example gets the point of both excitement and disbelief across with only two typeset characters, without any extra and frankly unnecessary words to explain our heroine's current mental state. Thankfully, the useful but admittedly quirky interrobang is not uncommon in children's books, so I decided to put it to good use. I settled on the less offensive "!?" version vice the "‽" version, which can't be found on any keyboard. *Yet.*

Made in the USA
Middletown, DE
26 October 2022